"A bad email reputation is like a hangover: hard to get rid of and it makes everything else hurt."

Christ Marriott

COPYRIGHT

Publisher: DJpressbooks

Published Date: 01-04-2023

Contact Information

DJPRESSBOOKS

dj press

EMAIL: djpressbooks@gmail.com

Book Design:
kandesigner@gmail.com

Simple Guide to Writing Professional Emails

Definitive Steps to Composing Winning Professional Emails to Get What You Want!

TABLE OF CONTENTS

Preface

Email has emerged as one of the main methods of communication in both personal and professional contexts in the current digital era. Despite its widespread use, many people have trouble creating emails that effectively and professionally express their intended message. This book fills that need.

The purpose of " Simple Guide to Writing Professional Emails" is to assist readers in creating emails that are precise, succinct, and successful in achieving their goals.

Introduction

"Simple Guide to Writing Professional Emails"

"The Definitive Steps to Composing Winning Professional Emails to Get What You Want"

Email is becoming a necessary tool for communication in both personal and professional contexts in the modern digital world. The ability to create emails that effectively express the intended message and tone is essential given the millions of emails sent and received daily.

"Simple Guide to Writing Professional Emails", seeks to offer helpful advice and pointers for crafting business emails that are effective. The guidelines and tactics presented in this book will assist you in writing clear and concise emails that accomplish your goals, whether you are speaking with coworkers, clients, or consumers.

You will learn how to structure your emails, pick the right terminology, and avert frequent errors through series of examples and activities. Also, you will learn how to avoid misunderstandings and misinterpretations by knowing the subtleties of email etiquette in a simplified way.

Anyone who wishes to improve their email writing abilities, from entry-level professionals to senior executives, should read and keep this book as their definitive guide. It is also appropriate for non-native English speakers who wish to improve their email writing skills.

"Simple Guide to Writing Professional Emails", will give you useful advice and techniques for writing emails that are crystal clear, concise, and polished whether you're a student, professional, or a business owner. You'll discover how to organize your emails, utilize appropriate syntax and punctuation, and develop an impactful message for your audience.

You will get helpful advice and examples in each chapter to guide you to become a better email writer. At the end of this book, you'll have the knowledge and assurance necessary to draft professional-looking emails that will get you what you want. Let us begin your road to mastering email communication, shall we?

The importance of Email Writing in Our Digital Age

The importance of email writing has always been an important element of our lives, especially in our professional lives. However, COVID-19 has accelerated the need and importance of professional emails as they have become the primary means of written communication. Everything that we now write is through email, and its benefit is immeasurable if written effectively.

Below are some of the benefits of emailing:

- It provides an easy referencing as it acts as a record keeper. You can keep a record of messages and replies, including details of when a message was received.

- It helps save time by just sending an email instead of setting up a face-to-face meeting with clients.

- It creates a professional image

- It enhances your credibility.

- It helps you build and maintain professional relationships.

- It communicates instantly

- It facilitates targeted communication.

- It can be accessed by anyone and will cost you nothing regardless of distance or the number of people involved.

Types of Emails

There are many types of emails and below are some examples that we encounter daily.

- Introduction letters
- Request letters
- Complaint letters
- Confirmation letters
- Agendas
- Enquiries
- Covering letters
- Minutes acceptance letters
- Job offers
- Report writing
- And more…

Styles of Emails

There are two email styles called **formal** and **informal** depending on the message's context and goal. Emails are frequently written in a formal tone that follows accepted corporate communication standards in professional settings. This affects the spelling and grammatical usage, courteous recipient etiquette, and the professional tone throughout the entire communication. While selecting the proper email style, it is essential to take the receiver and the message's context into account. An email that is properly written and adheres to the desired tone and purpose can improve communication and foster fruitful business partnerships. Hence, for effective communication, it is crucial to comprehend and use the correct email style depending of the purpose of your email.

➢ Formal Emails

Written communications known as formal emails often serve professional or commercial purposes and adhere to a set of conventions. They are often addressed to a someone in a position of power, such as a manager, a colleague, to a client, or customer. Professional emails need to be brief, precise, error-free, and written in a professional tone at all times. It's crucial to avoid using informal language or abbreviations while writing formal emails, as well as to use good grammar and punctuation.

➢ Informal Emails

Informal emails are often used for personal contact or for speaking with colleagues or friends informally. They differ from formal emails and are less structured and less official. Casual emails may have a less formal tone, include slang or acronyms, and employ less formal vocabulary. In contrast to professional emails, informal emails may not need a proper greeting or closure, and the subject line may be more humorous. It's crucial to keep in mind that even in a casual atmosphere, one should maintain respect and refrain from using unpleasant language or improper topics.

Example of an Informal Email

Subject: Weekend Plans

Hey Lea,

I just wanted to see what you have planned for this weekend and check. Any ideas? I'm considering visiting that brand-new eatery that just opened in the city. Want to come with me?

If you're available, let me know so we can work out the specifics.

Cheers,
Darren

Purpose of the Email

"Reaching the inbox isn't your goal - engaging people is"
Matt Blumberg

First, determine the purpose of the email as having a clear vision as to why you are writing will engage your audiance. Do you have to write this email? Could you have spoken to your colleague instead of writing an email?

The objective of the email should be obvious and precise, regardless of whether it is a formal or informal communication, to prevent misunderstandings. The main objective of an email is to accomplish a desired result, such as requesting action, eliciting a response, or sharing information.

In the end, an email's main goal is to engage the target audience and create positive interpersonal relationships. Therefore, you must ask yourself why you are writing this email. Examples of different purposes are given below, and we hope that they will be beneficial.

Why am I writing this email?

Am I **Confirming?**

- I am pleased to inform you that we have accepted your proposal.
- This email confirms my order for the...
- We would like to confirm that all the necessary information was given on...

Am I Responding?

- In response to your email dated...

- In replying to your email…
- I would like to take this opportunity to clarify the situation.
- We would like to give you the requested details of our new products…
- In response to your email dated...

Am **I Requesting?**

- Please send us your request as soon as possible...
- We would like to invite you to submit your request.
- Please send us your request at your earliest convenience.
- We would like to invite you to submit your request…

Am I **Enquiring?**

- Could you please send us your pricing structure?
- I am enquiring about your summer course dates...
- Could you please send us your delivery times?
- We are inquiring about your new café...

Am I **Complaining?**

- With reference to our recent purchase of the 50 laptops (purchase reference: 1234567),
- We would like to inform you that 20 out of the 50 laptops have a charging issue.

- I am deeply disappointed in...
- I regret that I must call your attention to...

Am I **Congratulating?**

- I would like to congratulate you on your recent promotion.
- We would like to congratulate you on your new baby.
- We would like to congratulate you on your recent successful project.
- We wish you all the best for your...
- I congratulate you on your early retirement.

Am I **Apologizing?**

- Please accept my sincere apologies for the misunderstanding or the mistake.

- We apologize for any inconvenience that this may cause/have caused.
- I apologize for the misunderstanding..
- Please accept our humble apology for the situation.
- I am so sorry to hear about…

Am I making a request?

- Please fill this form out by Friday the 15th to avoid.….
- Could you possibly arrange a team meeting for…
- If possible, could you send us the manuscript of the…
- We would indeed appreciate if you could…..
- Would you kindly respond to my email at your earliest?

Am I **replying to an email?**

- I would like to thank you for your email regarding…
- Thank you for getting back to me so quickly.
- In response to your request for the new computers….
- Attached are the requested documents of..

Am I **inviting?**

- You are warmly invited to...
- I would be delighted if you would join us for...
- We would appreciate if you could join us for...

Am **I just greeting to build a friendly rapport?**

- I hope this email finds you well.
- It was a pleasure meeting you at the….
- We are glad that we have got a chance to discuss about our upcoming…
- It was great to see you..

Am I asking questions?

- Could you please clarify the following points…
- Could you please send all the necessary information about…
- Please confirm if this marketing route is the final choice?
- Would you mind explaining the incident again?

Am I conveying information?

- Enclosed are the dates for our next courses.

- Attached is my CV for your consideration.

- I have enclosed all the requested contract documents.

The Four Decisive Keys In Effective Email Writing

Now that you have decided to write an email, consider the 4 decisive factors of email writing which are a set of principles and guidelines that can help you write more effective emails that get you what you want. These factors are writing; simple, polite, and short emails that contain accurate and all the necessary information.

Mastering these four decisive winning factors will distinguish you from others. As we now know the purpose of our email, writing effective emails is critical for conveying information, building relationships, and achieving desired outcomes.

Emails that are effective make it easier for readers to get to the point without much effort. By using the below four decsive keys as well as supportive structure will guide the reader to quickly receive the information they require and depart with it.

Key 1: Short Communication

It's crucial to get straight to the point in business emails, but it's also crucial to strike a balance between being too direct and overly wordy. First, make sure your email is organized with lots of white spaces. Nobody wants to read a big block of text, so reduce your paragraphs to a maximum of two or three phrases, and give each one enough room.

Key 2: Polite Communication

When communicating, the sender should be kind, polite, professional, truthful, enthusiastic, open, and thoughtful. Being polite requires that you are aware of both your own feelings and those of the other person. It also demonstrates your optimism and audience-centeredness, as the ultimate goal is to engage, not to disengage.

Key 3: Full Communication

Effective winning communication in emails depends on having a complete message. Providing the full message that has all the details the recipient needs to comprehend the message's context and goal is a winning factor. Include all the required email components, including a strong opening, a concise explanation of advantages, social proof, and a strong call to action. It would be unfortunate to lose a prospect because your footer or offer details were missing.

Key 4: Accurate Communication

Make sure that the information in the email is accurate to avoid embarrassments and law suits. Emails are legal records that can be used in a court of law. Also, in order to prevent misunderstandings and confusion, it's imperative that your emails contain the correct message, conveying to the recipient what you intend to say. Communication can break down when an error is made in a message, such as a misspelling or inaccurate information, and the recipient may understand the message differently than it was intended to be understood. This may cause pointless follow-up emails or even harm business relationships. Before sending your email, make sure it is thoroughly proofread to make sure the message is correct, clear, and error-free. Verifying your message, a second time can help you communicate more effectively and positively by saving time and avoiding confusion.

10 Winning Steps of Email Structure

Effective email writing requires a solid understanding of email structure. In this section, 10 simple winning steps are offered with examples that will be your ultimate guide. The recipient may find it simpler to comprehend an email that is well-structured and to respond accordingly.

A winning structure of an email includes the following elements: a clear purpose that analyzes the receivers and their needs; a clear and concise subject line; a correct greeting; an opening sentence that introduces the purpose of the email; the main body of the email that provides the details and supporting information; a conclusion that states what are your desired outcomes; a polite closing; and your name and contact information.

STEP 1: Who Is The Receiver of The Email?

This is due to the fact that the average person receives 90 emails every day. In order to customize your message to your audience and make sure that it is appropriate for the receiver, it is crucial to know who you are writing to in an email. Being aware of your audience will help you select the right amount of specificity and tone for your email and reduce the likelihood of misunderstandings. Last but not least, sending the email to the appropriate recipient will ensure that it is read by them and will prevent you from providing private or sensitive material to the wrong person. Below are some practical examples that you can take onboard.

- Did you check that you have the correct email address of the receiver?
- Is there someone with a similar email address/names that you have to be careful of?
- Did you check the correct spelling of their name and their title? For a known receiver: Dr./Mr./Ms./Mrs./Miss
- For an unknown receiver: To whom it may concern: Dear Sir/Madam
- Is the receiver interested in the subject?
- Is the receiver familiar with your views?
- Does the receiver trust your judgment on the subject or speaks a different language from you?
- If previously dealt with, what kind of approach usually appeals to them?

STEP 2: Title / Subject Line

When someone receives your email, the subject line is the first thing they see which can be interpreted as the entrance door of the email. The recipient's attention can be drawn and persuaded to read more of your email with the help of a clear, concise subject line that appropriately summarizes the substance of your email.

Examples

- Weekly team meeting

- Grades release date
- Exam dates

- Request for an emergency meeting
- Incident Report

- Application for…

- Please aknowledge receipt of this email

STEP 3: Greeting

Since it sets the tone for the entire email, a greeting is a must for business emails. Creating a positive rapport with the recipient through a thoughtful greeting may be crucial for attaining the outcomes you desire. The greeting should represent the right amount of formality for the circumstance and be customized to your relationship with the recipient.

- If you are writing to a manager, director, or senior executive, you may use a more formal greeting, such as "Dear Mr. or Mrs. [Last Name],"
- If you are writing to a colleague, you could use a more informal greeting, such as "Hello [First Name]".
- If the recipient has a particular title, then make sure of that you include the title. Using the right greeting builds a good rapport and trust as it shows that you have considered their relationship with you, their position, and rank.
- The lack of a greeting can be perceived as a show of contempt in some cultures since it is valued more highly than it is in other cultures. As a result, it's also crucial to consider cultural variations while selecting your greeting.

STEP 4: Opening Sentences / Introduction

The purpose of the email should be stated clearly and concisely in the introduction, which is the opening sentence. This clarifies the purpose of the email for the reader. Remember that your purpose is to get that message across easily and clearly, not as a show of your language ability or a power trip. It demonstrates that you have given the recipient's needs some thought, that you value and appreciate their time and attention. An effective beginning can influence the reader favorably and give them a positive first impression of you as a communicator.

Examples

- I'm writing to inquire about..

- We would like to inquire about
- With reference to your email dated...

- Further to the out-of-zoom meeting
- I would like to request...

- Further to our telephone conversation,...
- Further to our discussion...
- I would like to thank you for the offer.

STEP 5: Body of The Email

The details and supporting material that the receiver needs to comprehend your message should be included in the email body. It is the most important component of the communication and the core of your email. You can set the scene, describe your email's intent, include pertinent data that backs up your case, and provide the context of the email. It also gives you a chance to establish a rapport with the recipient and show off your professionalism and knowledge.

Moreover, the email body gives you the opportunity to communicate your point in a simple, direct, and interesting way. You may help the recipient grasp your message and respond correctly by structuring your thoughts and information in a logical and simple style. Using facts and data as evidence to support your opening statement can influence the recipient to achieve your desired outcome.

Examples

- We would appreciate it if you would send us all the necessary information on your products and advertised services.

- I am pleased to inform you that you have been selected for the second round of interviews and would like you to bring all your certificates next week on the…..

STEP 6: Conclusion

A strong email conclusion can enhance the message's overall efficacy, among other advantages. The conclusion should include a call-to-action that tells the recipient what you want them to do next. This is to reaffirm the email's main idea, highlight its most important parts, and leave the reader with positive feelings. Furthermore, a strong conclusion can demonstrate expertise and attention to detail, which will help to build your trust and reputation.

Examples

- If you require any further information, feel free to call me at...
- I look forward to hearing from you soon.
- We would be grateful if you could get in touch with us before the end of the month.
- We would like you to refund our money as the product is faulty.
- Please make sure that the pricing of the new product is completed before our weekly team meeting.
- We would appreciate it if you could fix the electric wiring of the building within the agreed time, which is Wednesday, June 5.
- I look forward to your early reply.
- We look forward to working with you.

STEP 7: Closure

Professionalism, clarity, and courtesy in communicating are the keys to successfully ending emails. You can make sure that your emails are efficient, interesting, and leave the recipient with a good impression by adhering to these suggestions.

Make sure that you use a suitable and professional closing for your emails.

Examples:

- "Regards," "Best regards,"
- "Sincerely," "Faithfully,"
- "Warm Regards," or "Thank you."
- Yours Faithfully: formal (Name unknown)
- Yours sincerely: very formal, already used in email correspondence (name known).

STEP 8: Signature

An email signature is a small paragraph of text at the end of the email. It often includes the sender's name, job title, business name, and contact information, including a phone number, email address, and website. Even if the recipient already knows who you are, you still have to sign off with your complete name in every email you send.

An email signature may also contain a quote, a call to action, or links to social media accounts in addition to the sender's contact details. To avoid detracting from the message's substance, the email signature should be kept straightforward and uncluttered. Ultimately, a well-designed email signature can help develop a professional image and improve communication. Make sure your signature block is up-to-date before pressing the Send button because your recipient will think that he or she can use any information provided, just like on a real business card.

Ms. Sarah Adams
Human Resources Director, FEDX
Email:admsarah@fedex.com.uk
www.perfectwritecommunity.co.uk
+44-7076737356

STEP 9: Editing

Editing is crucial because it gives you the chance to improve your writing and make sure that you are sending the intended message. By doing this, the sender and recipient may avoid misunderstandings and improper communication. In this step you will identify, then edit any mistakes making your written communication clear in order to serve its purpose.

Editing Checklist

- Have you used paragraphing?
- Is the email address the correct one?
- Check your sentence structure
- Check the spelling, especially the spelling of the receiver's name.
- Check the punctuation.
- Check if your language is inclusive.
- Check if you have repeated words, and if you do, remove or replace them.
- Check your email subject line.
- Check that you have used the correct greetings.
- Check that you have an excellent opening sentence.
- Check that your email body is explaining all the details.
- Check that your conclusion says the outcome that you want to see happen.
- Check that you have used the correct closing.
- Check that you have confirmed your position and company signature.

STEP 10: Proofreading

Proofreading is a very important part of reviewing your email before you hit send. In this process, we perfect our written communication to make sure of its accuracy, readability, professional image, and clarity to prevent misunderstandings.

Also, proofreading emails might assist in identifying any mistakes or typos that might have escaped notice during the first drafting stage. This ensures that the email seems polished and professional. Last but not least, spending the time to modify an email demonstrates to the receiver that the sender respects and values their attention.

The 10 Simple Winning Steps in Email Writing Table

This simple table can be printed, put next to your computer/laptop and used as a guide. If you follow these steps correctly, there will be no doubt that your email will be a winning professional email that will get you what you want and build a professional image.

1 Who	**2** Subject
3 Greeting	**4** Opening Sentences
5 Body	**6** Conclusion
7 Closure	**8** Signature
9 Editing	**10** Proofreading

Oxford Comma

The Oxford comma, commonly referred to as the serial comma, is a punctuation mark used after the penultimate item in a list of three or more items. By distinctly dividing the list's contents, it helps to eliminate ambiguity and make a sentence's meaning more obvious. The Oxford University Press, where it has historically been employed, is where the Oxford comma gets its name. Its use is a matter of taste and preference, however it is frequently advised in academic writing and journalism to minimize confusion. While some style manuals, like the AP Stylebook, forbid the use of the Oxford comma, others, like the Chicago Manual of Style, do. The Oxford comma should ultimately be used depending on the writer's personal writing style and the target audience.

The second-to-last item in a list of three or more items should be followed by an Oxford comma, sometimes known as a serial comma. By distinctly separating the list's contents, it serves the function of preventing ambiguity in sentences. Take the phrase "I asked my parents, Rory and Reem to supper,". Without the Oxford comma, it can be taken to mean that Rory and Reem are my parents. It should be as follows: I invited my parents, Rory, and Reem to dinner. With the Oxford comma, it would be evident that I the speaker invited four individuals.

The usage of the Oxford comma is a contentious issue among authors and editors since some think it is unnecessary for good writing while others think it is necessary. Oxford comma proponents contend that it enhances clarity and uniformity in writing, particularly in academic or technical writing where accuracy is crucial..

The Oxford comma is still a widely used punctuation mark in English writing despite the controversy surrounding it. In many academic and publishing situations, it is favoured and frequently used in American English.

Due to a missing Oxford comma in their employment contract, the Maine-based Oakhurst Dairy lost a lawsuit in 2018 and was forced to pay their delivery drivers $5 million in overtime pay. It was unclear whether the drivers were entitled to overtime compensation for chores like packing, which was not specifically included in the contract, as a result of the absence of the Oxford comma. The corporation suffered a large financial loss as a result of the court's decision that the contract was unclear and took the drivers' side. This situation emphasizes the value of language clarity and the potential repercussions of skipping or incorrectly employing punctuation, such as the Oxford comma.

Examples of Oxford Comma

- We visited London, Leeds, and Colchester on our UK trip.
- The members are made up of faculty, staff, and students.
- Her favorite colors are black, white, and brown.
- I ordered a burger, a salad, and a soup.
- Our project team includes, designers, administrators, and project managers.
- My grocery list includes grapes, peanuts, and bread.

Email etiquette summarised

Communication is the cornerstone of any great Organization. **Good Communication** leads to great collaboration, a healthy corporate environment and a well consolidated effort towards a common goal. Emails are an important part of this communication chain. Email Etiquette provides a set of guidelines that one should follow to communicate better.

- Get the Content right.
- Get the right subject line, greeting, body of the email, conclusion, and closure.
- Get the right tone and Language.
- Get the right structure of your email.
- Get your Email formatted to an acceptable standard

DO S and DON'TS

There are many dos and don’ts when writing a professional email, but we will focus on the core ones that should be considered.

DOs

- Stay objective; no feelings, opinions, or reflexions included.
- Make sure that your email address is a professional one that reflects your real name, correct titles, not a nick name.
- Make your subject clear and concise
- Avoid abbreviations while being professional and respectful.
- Proofread your email to remove typos, spelling and grammar mistakes, and unclear statements.
- Get straight to the point and make sure your message is clear and concise.
- Make sure that you use a professional email signature.
- Make sure that you put a comma between the month and the year only when the day is mentioned. Monday, March 2, 2023
- Use; Dear Mr., Ms., or Mrs, when first contacting a person
- Use; Dear Sir/Madam for when the recipient is unknown.
- Use the Oxford Comma to avoid ambiguities.

DON'T

- Write in an informal way, regardless of your relationship with the receiver.
- Assume that the receiver knows who you are and fully understands the topic that you are writing about.
- Use emoticons
- Give repetitive information
- Put a comma between the month and year when a day is not mentioned. August 2023
- Use capital letters for the whole email or excessive punctuation is considered as aggressive and shouting.
- Include personal information or be subjective.
- Use abbreviations or slang.
- Use inappropriate language that can be interpreted as unprofessional or disrespectful.
- Use email as a substitute for face-to-face communication.
- Send your email without reading it to yourself to feel the tone of the message.
- Send the email before you have checked the correct email of the recipient (same names, titles).

Examples of Emails

EXAMPLE EMAIL 1

SUBJECT: Complaint- Poor Customer Service

GREETING: Dear Mr Adam John,

INTRODUCTION: I am writing to express my disappointment with the service I received from your customer service team on 28 Sept 2022, due to an issue that I had with a cupboard that I bought from your store.

BODY: I bought the cupboard (model: 4668-78-) on the 25th of March and when brought to my house, it couldn't be assembled using the provided tools that it came with. When I contacted your company, I was met with unprofessionalism and incompetence and even refused to at least trobleshoot. The representative I spoke to was rude and unhelpful and were not able to provide me with a solution.

CONCLUSION: I would appreciate it if you could investigate this matter, take the necessary steps to ensure that I either get a replacement or refund for the cupboard within seven days.

CLOSURE: Regards,
SIGNATURE: Ms. Sarah Adams
Human Resources Director,
FEDX Email:admsarah@fedex.com.uk
www.perfectwritecommunity
+44-7076737356

EXAMPLE EMAIL 2

SUBJECT: Enquiry about the New English Summer Course

GREETING: Dear Course Coordinator,

INTRODUCING THE PURPOSE: I hope this email finds you well. I am writing to enquire about your new English Summer Course. I am interested in pursuing this course and would appreciate it if you could provide me with some information about it.

MAIN BODY: Firstly, I would like to know the admission requirements, the fees, the duration of the course and the start dates for the upcoming sessions. Secondly, could you please provide me with the details of the curriculum, including the topics that will be covered and the skills that will be developed through the course? I would like to know about the credentials of the faculty members who will be teaching the course and their experience in the field.

CONCLUSION: I appreciate your time and assistance in providing me with the above information in the coming days so that I don't miss the summer program.

CLOSURE: Thank you,
SIGNATURE: Mr Dereck James
Email: derekjames@fedex.com.uk
www.perfectwritecommunity
Tel: +44-7076737356

EXAMPLE EMAIL 3

SUBJECT: Product Prices inquiry

GREETING: Dear Amazon Customer Service,

INTRODUCTION: I am writing to inquire about your current prices of the iPhone 12 and iPhone 13.

BODY: Could you please provide me with the price list of the phones? I would also like to know if there are any ongoing promotions or discounts available, payment methods, and shipping options.

CONCLUSION: I look forward to hearing from you soon.

CLOSURE: Thank you,

SIGNATURE: Ms Deema Ahmed
Email: Deemahedh@fedex.com.uk
Web: www.perfectwritecommunity
Tel: +44-7076737356

EXAMPLE EMIAL 4

SUBJECT: Congratulations!

GREETING: Dear [Colleague's Name],

OPENING: We just wanted to take a moment to congratulate you on your recent promotion. It is well deserved and a testament to your hard work and dedication to our company.

BODY: We are thrilled to see you achieve this milestone in your career, and I have no doubt that you will excel in your new role. Please know that I am here to support you in any way I can.

CONCLUSION: Once again, congratulations on your well-deserved promotion.

CLOSURE: Best regards,

SIGNATURE: Mrs Hana Avery
Email: Harreit@fedex.com.uk
Web: www.perfectwritecommunity
Tel: +44-7076737786

EXAMPLE EMAIL 5

SUBJECT: Apology for Order Delay

GREETING: Dear [Name of the Customer],

OPENING: I am writing to sincerely apologize for the delay in processing and shipping your order. We understand that this has caused you inconvenience and frustration, and we are deeply sorry for any inconvenience we may have caused.

BODY: We encountered an unexpected delay in our production process, which caused the delay in processing your order. However, I want to assure you that we are doing everything we can to expedite the process and have your order shipped as soon as possible.

CONCLUSION: If you have any questions or concerns regarding your order, please feel free to contact us. We will be happy to assist you in any way we can.

Again, please accept our sincere apologies for the delay in processing and shipping your order. Thank you for your continued support and understanding.

CLOSURE: Best regards,

SIGNATURE: Mr Jack Wyat
Email: Harreit@fedex.com.uk
Web: www.perfectwritecommunity
Tel: +44-7076737786

EXAMPLE EMAIL 6

SUBJECT: Request for Information

GREETING: Dear [Recipient's Name],

OPENING: We hope this email finds you well. We are writing to request some information regarding your new aple product. We are interested in learning more about those new tablets.

BODY: We are wondering if you could provide us all the product specifications, prices, sales, and your delivery schedule.

CONCLUSION: I would be grateful if you could share all the relevant information or point us in the direction of any helpful resources about the new apple tablets.

Thank you for your time and assistance. We look forward to hearing back from you soon.

CLOSURE: Best regards,

SIGNATURE: Mr Garry Grayson
Email: Harreit@fedex.com.uk
Web: www.perfectwritecommunity
Tel: +44-70345737786

EXAMPLE EMAIL 7

SUBJECT: Order Confirmation: (64587739-77)

GREETING: Dear Ms Johnson,

OPENING: We would like to thank you for placing an order with us. We are delighted to inform you that your order has been received and confirmed.

BODY: Your order has been processed and will be shipped within the next three business days. We will send you a confirmation email with the shipping details once your order has been dispatched.

CONCLUSION: If you have any questions or concerns regarding your order, please feel free to contact us.

CLOSURE: Best regards,

SIGNATURE: Mrs Harreit Harper
Email: Harreit@fedex.com.uk
Web: www.perfectwritecommunity
Tel: +9665502764565

Conclusion

This is a simple definitive guide to composing a winning email that will help you get what you want. In reading this book, you will greatly enhance your email writing abilities on email writing as a resource. It covers simple crucial subjects including appropriate email format, structure, language, tone, and etiquette, along with useful pointers for enhancing your writing style. You can write emails that are clear, concise, and compelling by using the principles and strategies described in the book. By doing so, you will become a more successful communicator and raise your chances of success in both your personal and professional lives.

This book offered simple instructions and resources that you need to create interesting and persuasive emails, whether you're a student, a professional, or just someone who wants to communicate more effectively. Therefore, you will be able to build mastery skills in writing professional winning emails that will get you what you want.

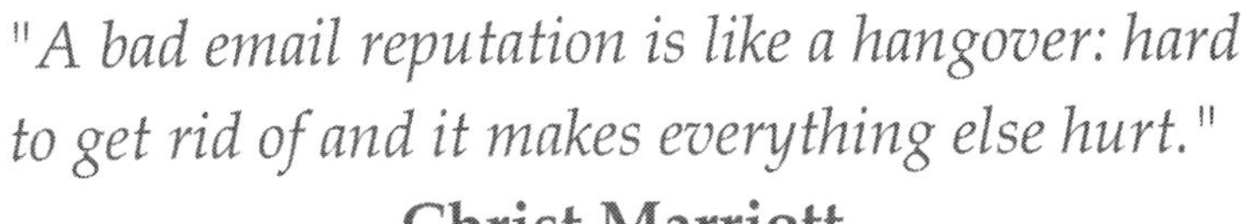

"A bad email reputation is like a hangover: hard to get rid of and it makes everything else hurt."

Christ Marriott

Simple Guide to Writing Professional Emails

Definitive Steps to Composing Winning Professional Emails to Get What You Want!

Contact Information

DJPRESSBOOKS

EMAIL: djpressbooks@gmail.com

Made in the USA
Las Vegas, NV
28 October 2023